CONTENTS

25.RUSSIAN CICADA - P28

26.JACK O' LANTERN CASE (HAT) - P29

27.BROOM - P30

28.JACK O' LANTERN - P31

26.WITCH - P32

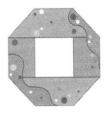

27.DOUGHNUT - P33

28.LENGTH SAMURAI HAT - P34

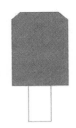

29.LOLLYPOP - P35

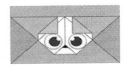

30.DOG'S LETTER - P36

31.FAMILY HEART - P37

32.BALLOON WITH WINGS - P38

33.CAT - P39

33.GORILLA - P40

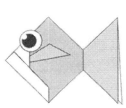

34.GOLDFISH - P41

35.SIAMESE CAT - P42

36.PINEAPPLE - P43

37.PANSY - P44

38.MUSHROOM - P45

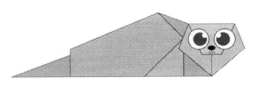

39.SEA DOG - P46

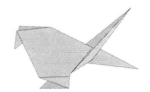

40.TWEETY BIRD - P47

41.BLACK CAT - P48

42.SUNFLOWER - P49

43.COASTER - P50

SYMBOLS

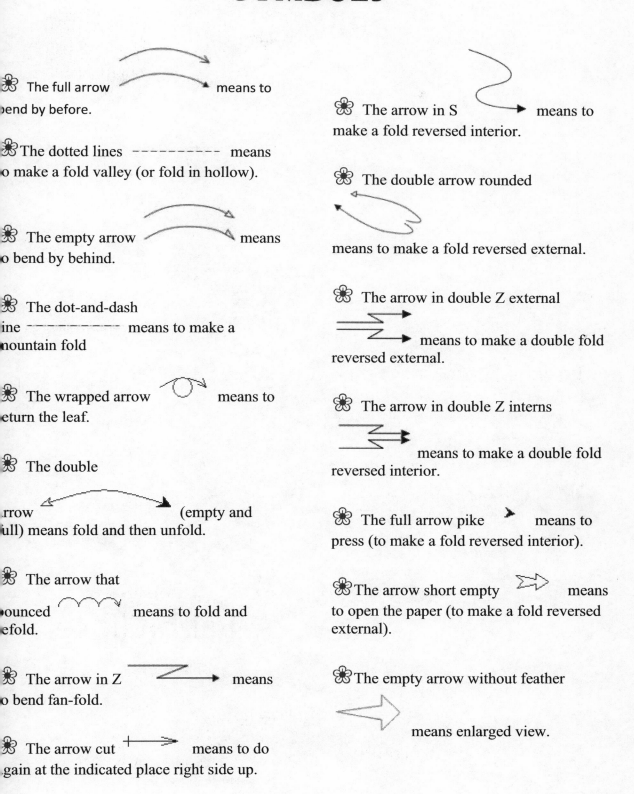

❀ The full arrow ⌒ means to bend by before.

❀ The dotted lines – – – – – – means to make a fold valley (or fold in hollow).

❀ The empty arrow ⌒ means to bend by behind.

❀ The dot-and-dash line –·–·–·–·– means to make a mountain fold

❀ The wrapped arrow ↺ means to return the leaf.

❀ The double arrow (empty and full) means fold and then unfold.

❀ The arrow that bounced ⌒⌒⌒ means to fold and refold.

❀ The arrow in Z ⟋ means to bend fan-fold.

❀ The arrow cut ⊢→ means to do again at the indicated place right side up.

❀ The arrow in S ⟿ means to make a fold reversed interior.

❀ The double arrow rounded ⟲ means to make a fold reversed external.

❀ The arrow in double Z external ⟾ means to make a double fold reversed external.

❀ The arrow in double Z interns ⟾ means to make a double fold reversed interior.

❀ The full arrow pike ➤ means to press (to make a fold reversed interior).

❀ The arrow short empty ⇨ means to open the paper (to make a fold reversed external).

❀ The empty arrow without feather ⇨ means enlarged view.

RABBIT

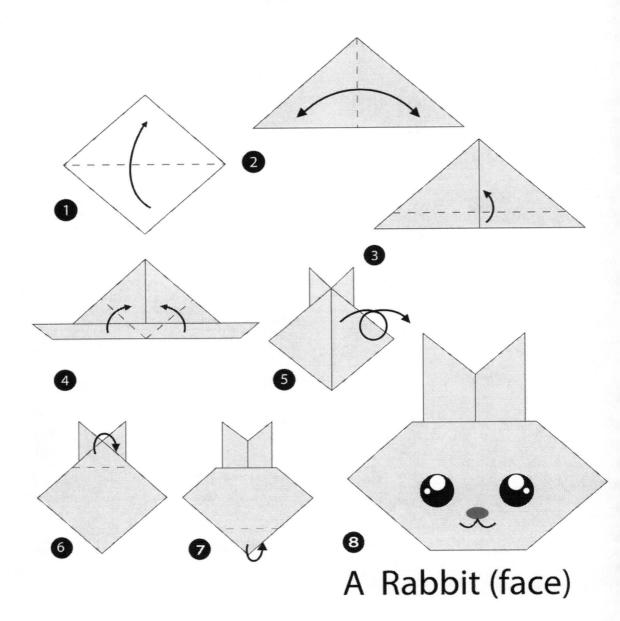

A Rabbit (face)

HORSE

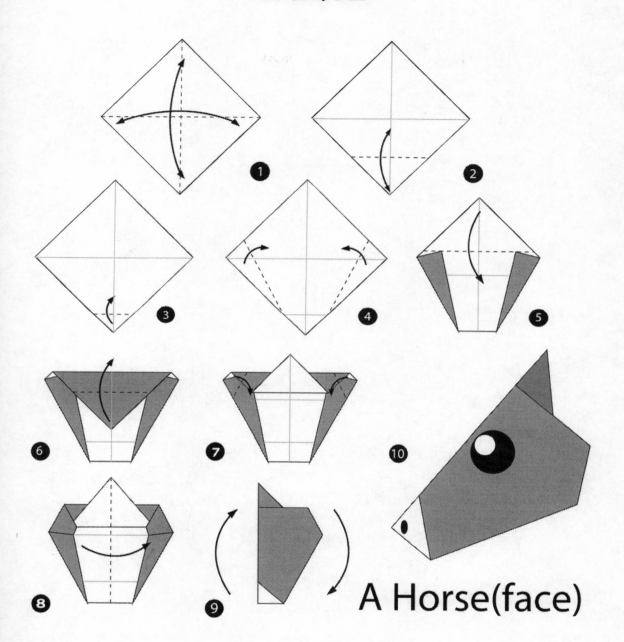

A Horse(face)

BIRD

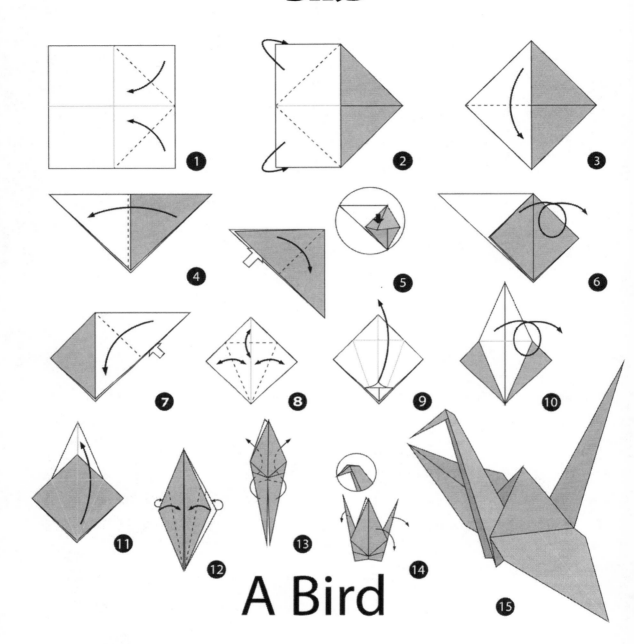

A Bird

PIGEON

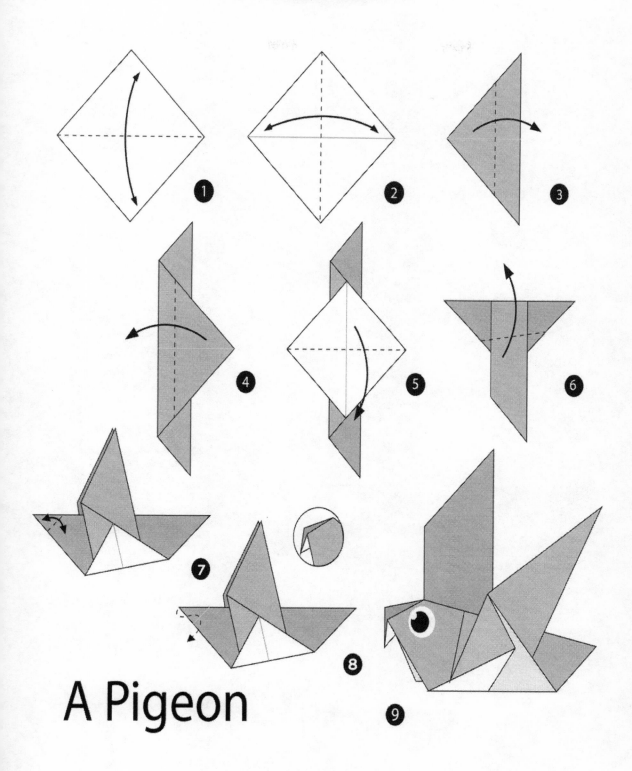

A Pigeon

ELEPHANT

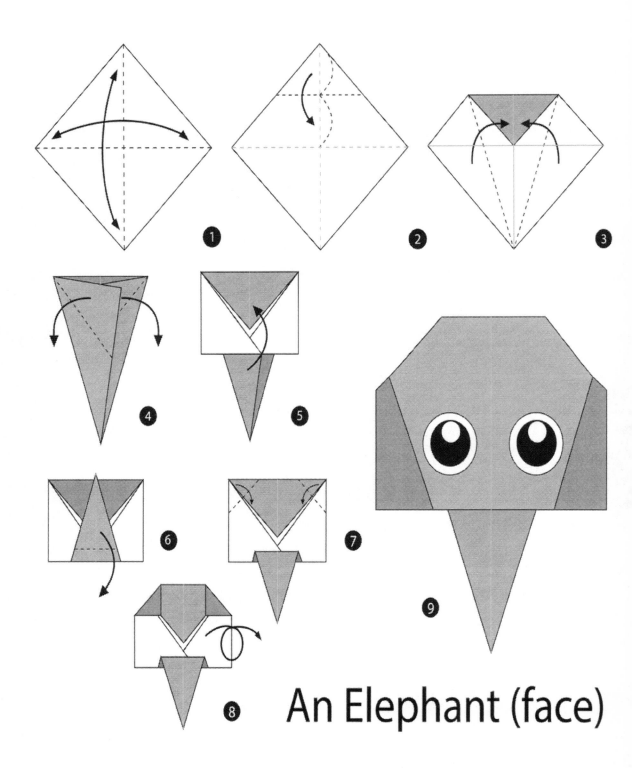

An Elephant (face)

8

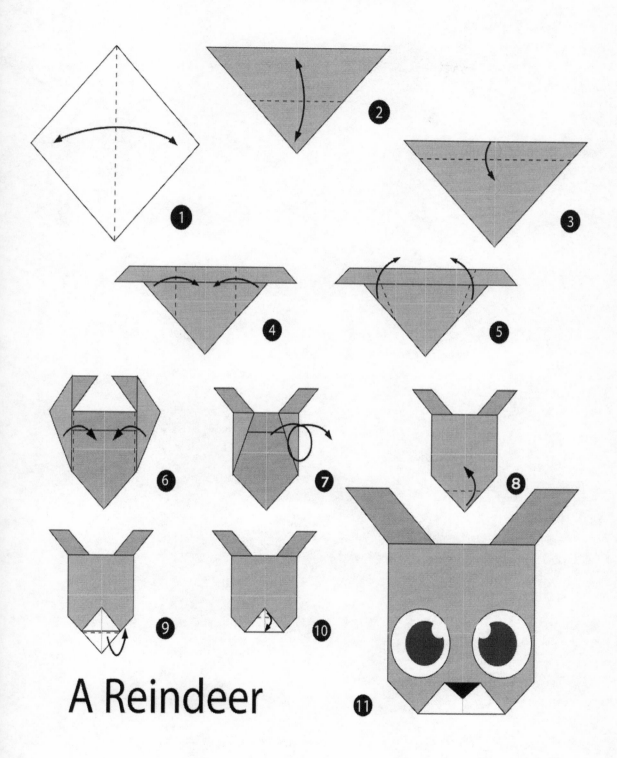

A Reindeer

BIRD

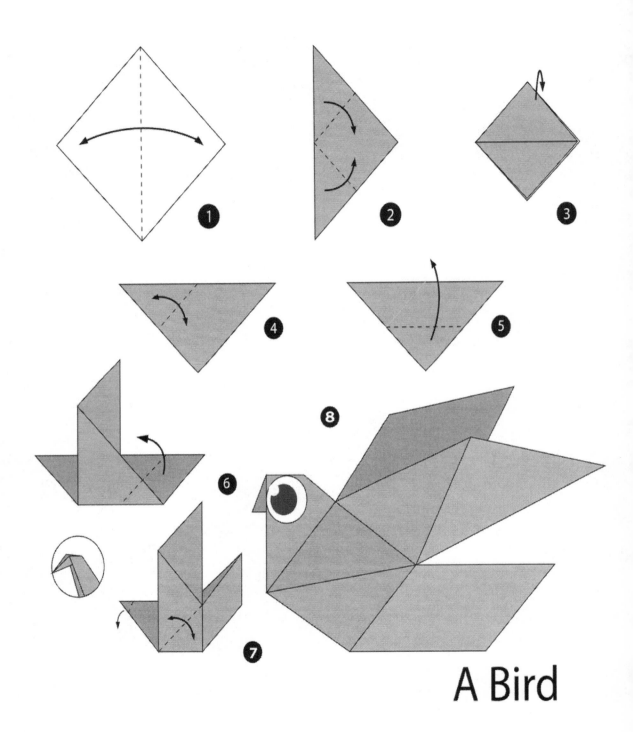

1

2

3

4

5

6

7

8

A Bird

CRAWLING CROW

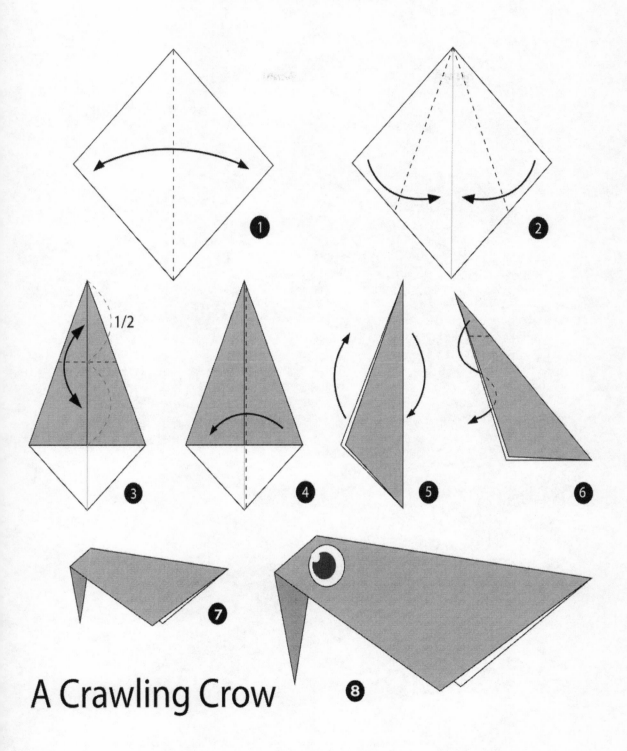

A Crawling Crow

SEA LION

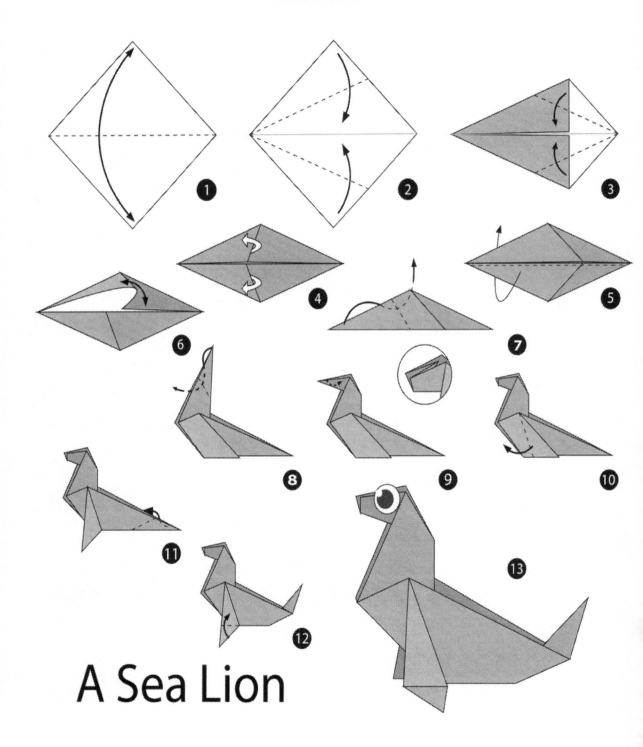

A Sea Lion

SPARROW

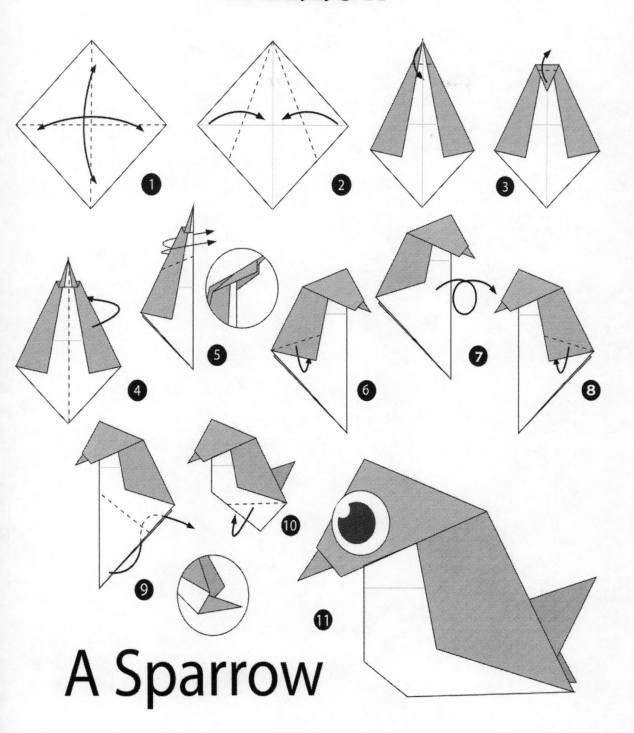

A Sparrow

GIRAFFE

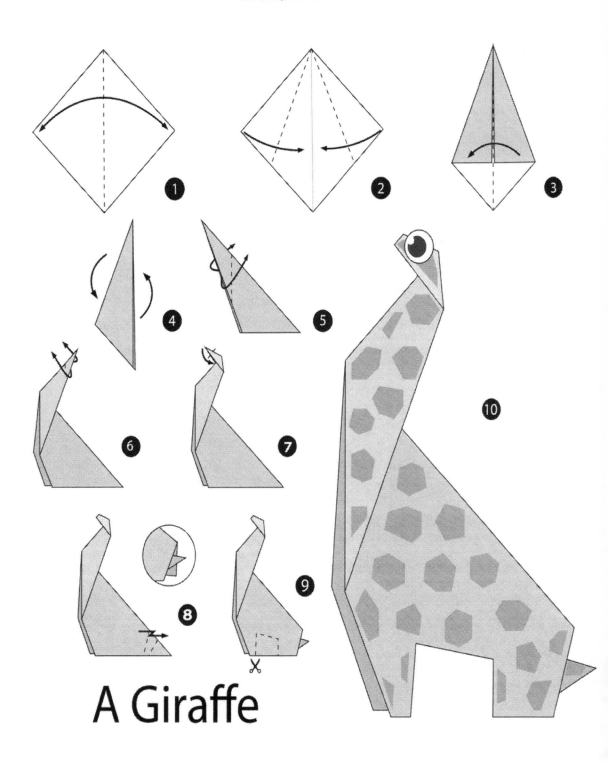

1

2

3

4

5

6

7

8

9

10

A Giraffe

CROCODILE

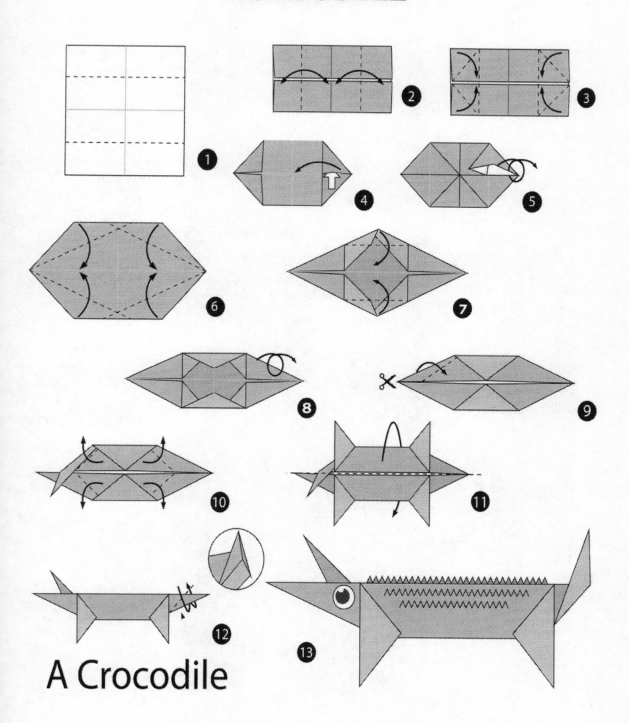

A Crocodile

CRAB

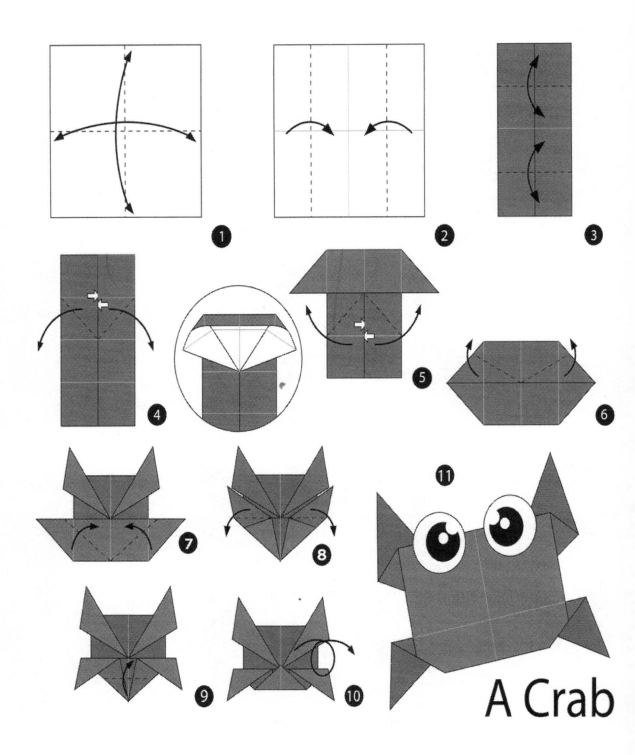

A Crab

PENGUIN

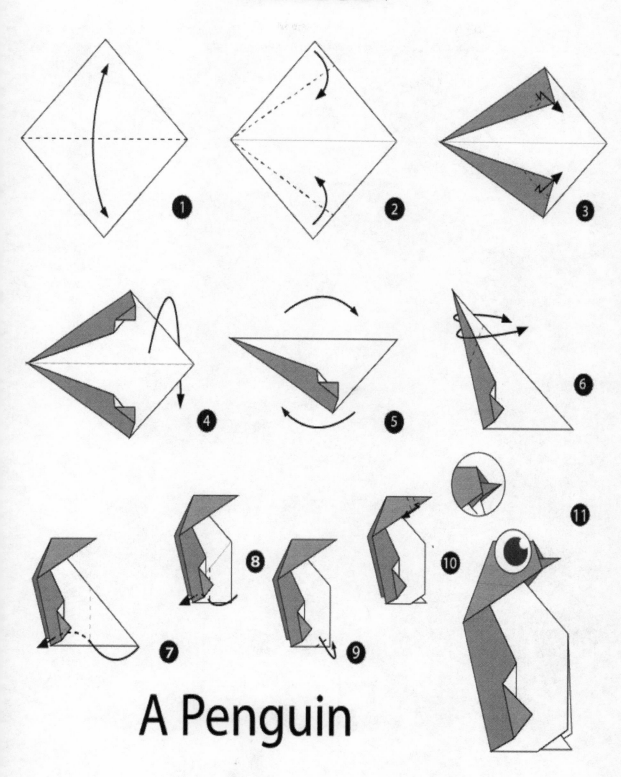

A Penguin

BIRD

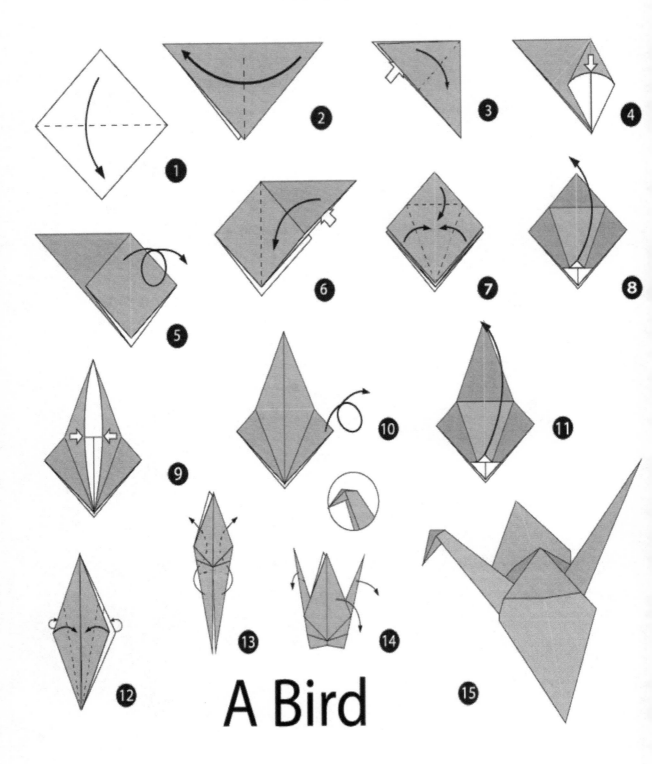

A Bird

BUTTERFLY

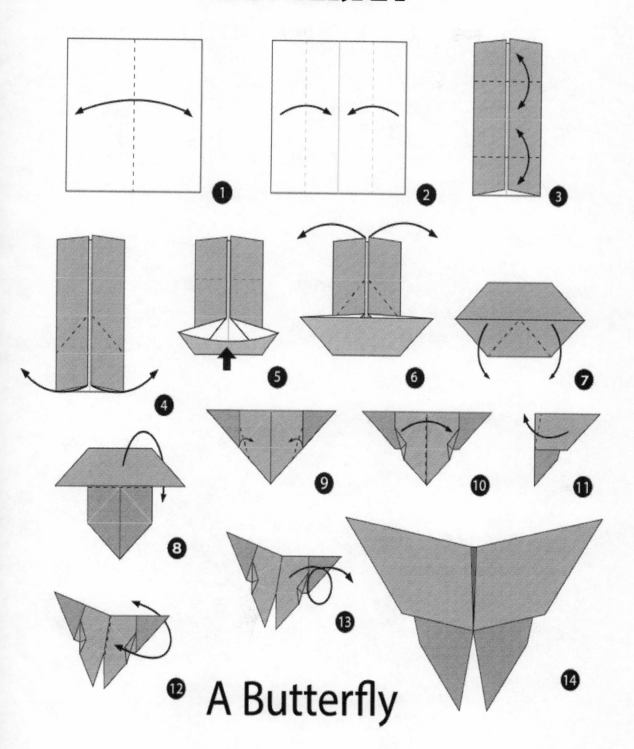

A Butterfly

TYRANNOSAURUS

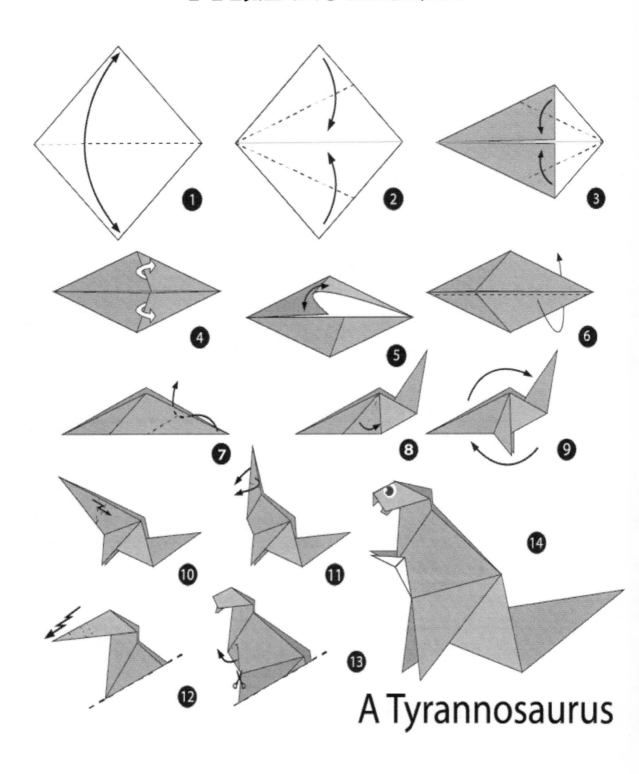

A Tyrannosaurus

RABBIT

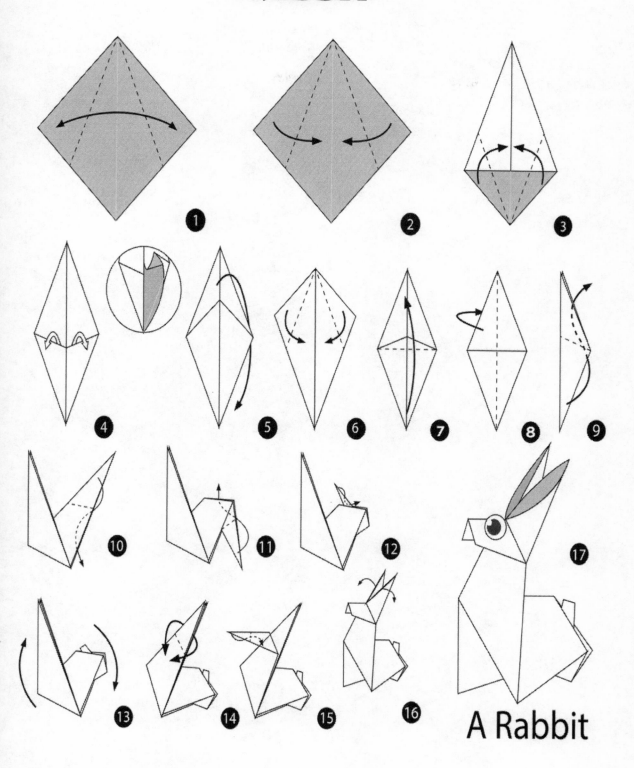

A Rabbit

PARROT

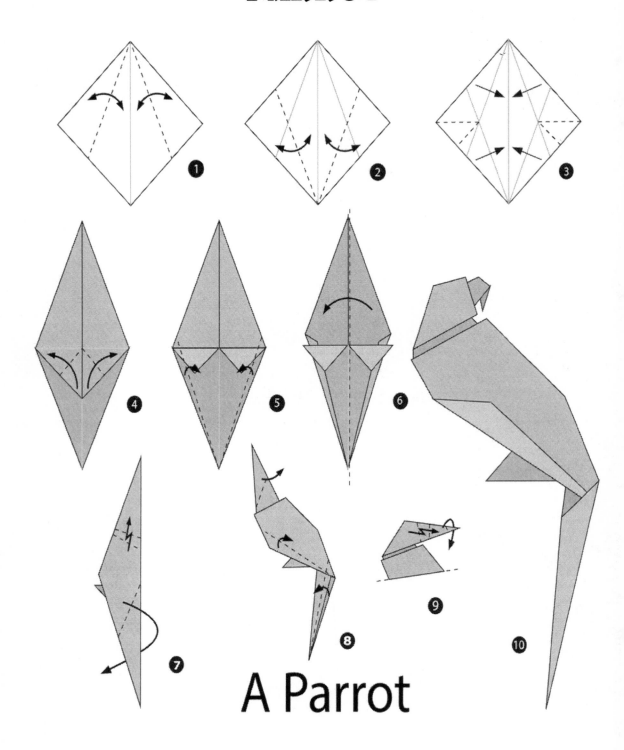

A Parrot

CROAKING FROG

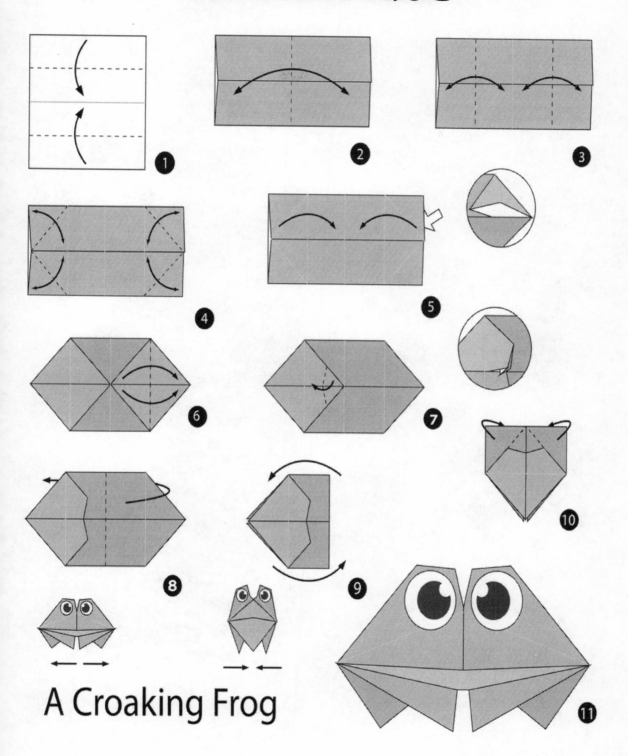

A Croaking Frog

ELEPHANT

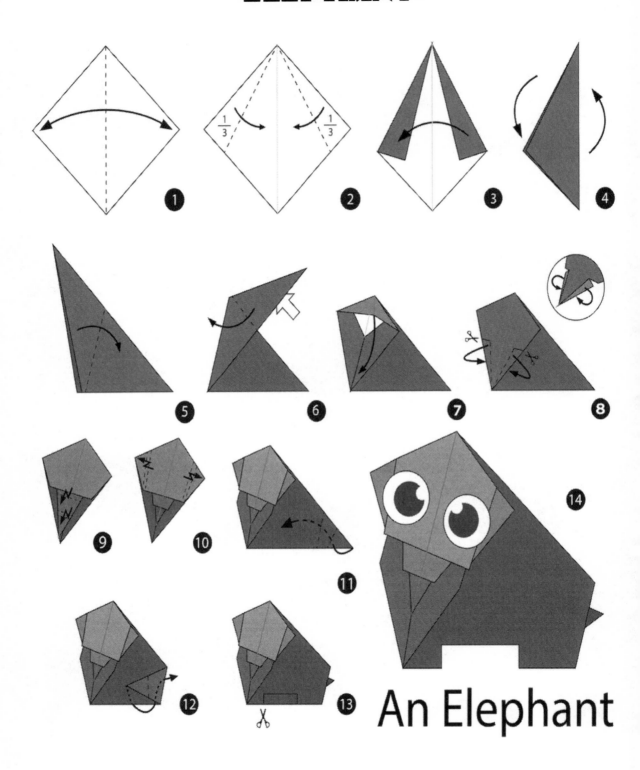

An Elephant

MOUSE

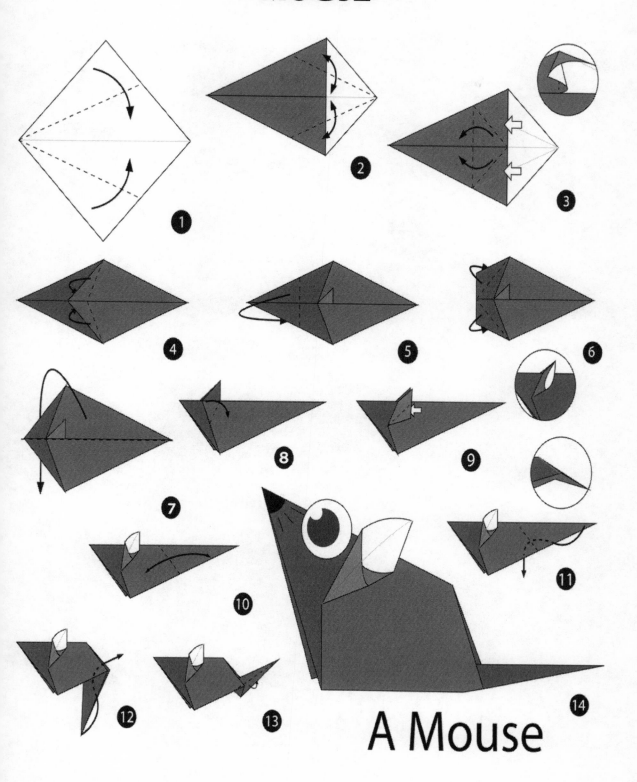

A Mouse

25

JUMPING FROG

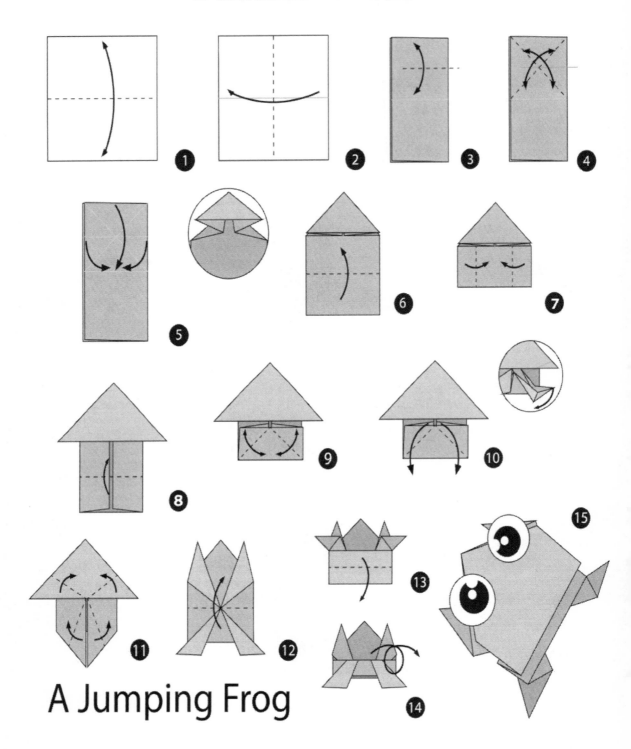

A Jumping Frog

BUTTERFLY

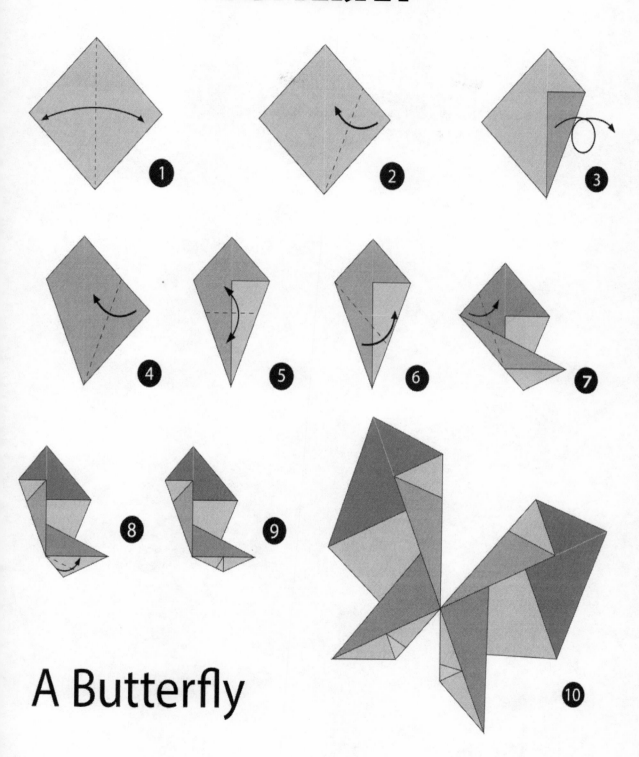

A Butterfly

RUSSIAN CICADA

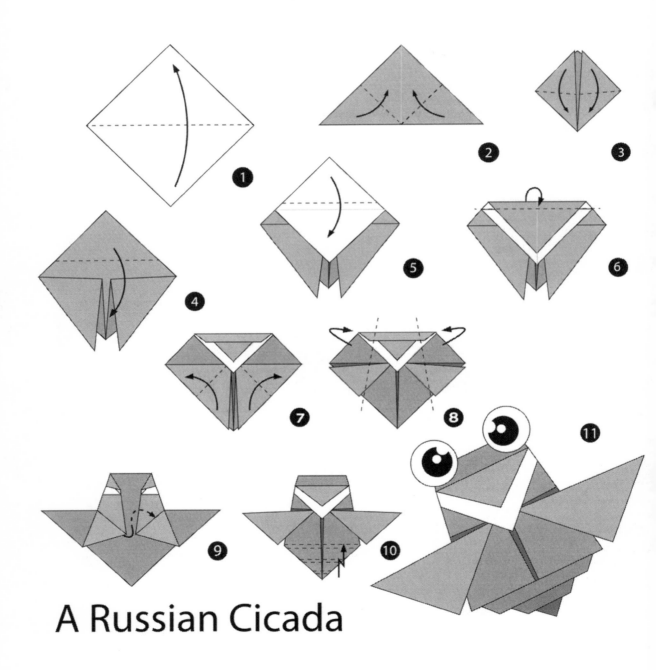

A Russian Cicada

JACK O' LANTERN CASE

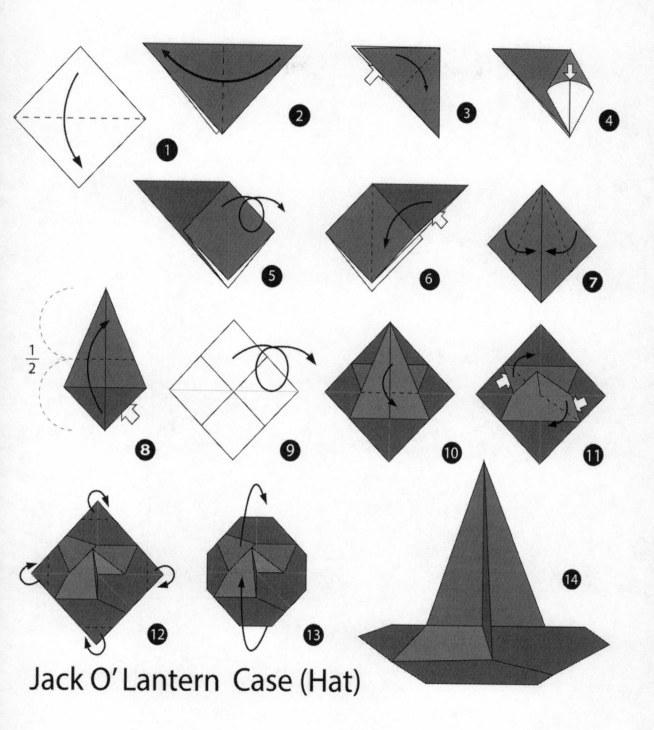

Jack O' Lantern Case (Hat)

BROOM

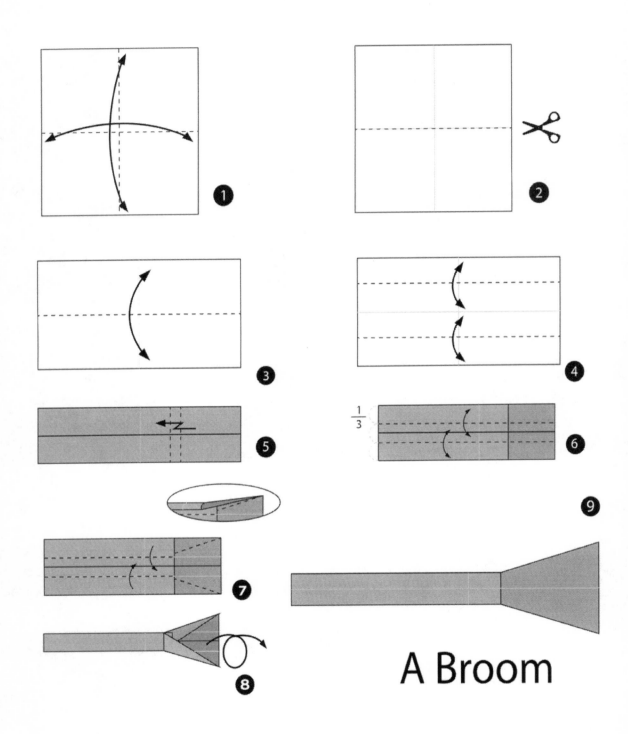

A Broom

JACK O' LANTERN

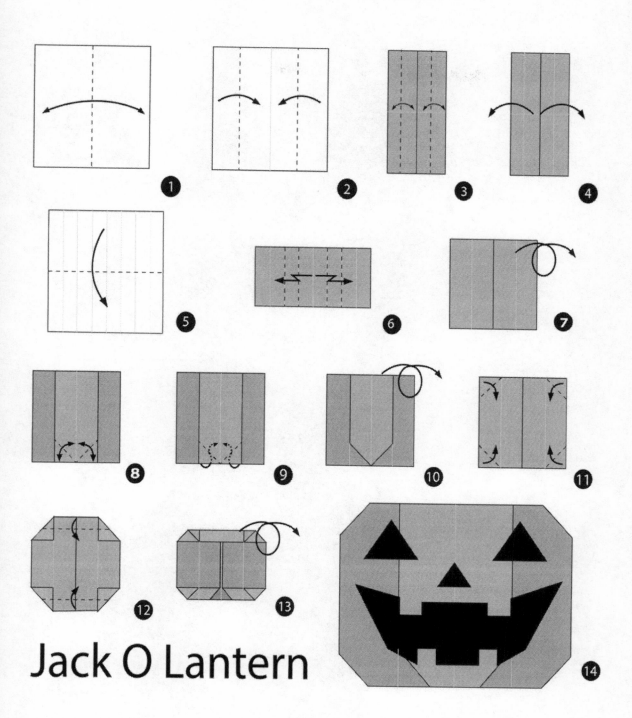

Jack O Lantern

WITCH

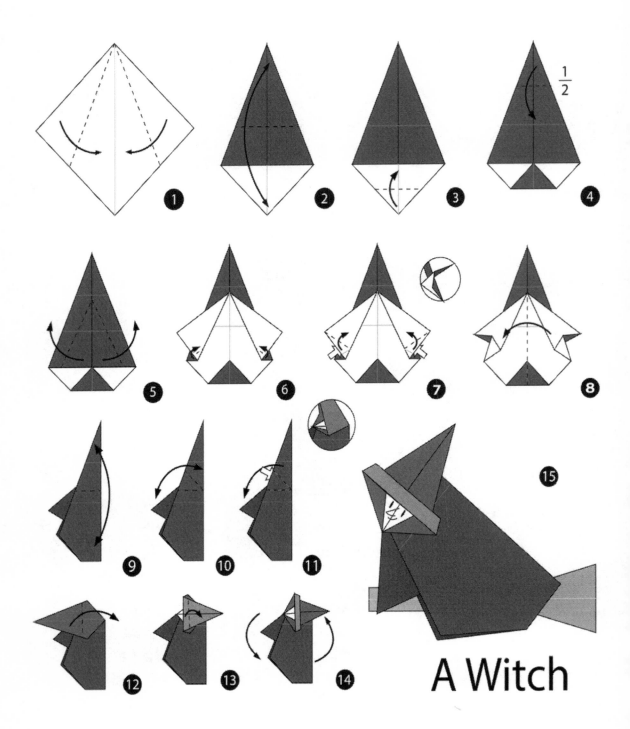

A Witch

DOUGHNUT

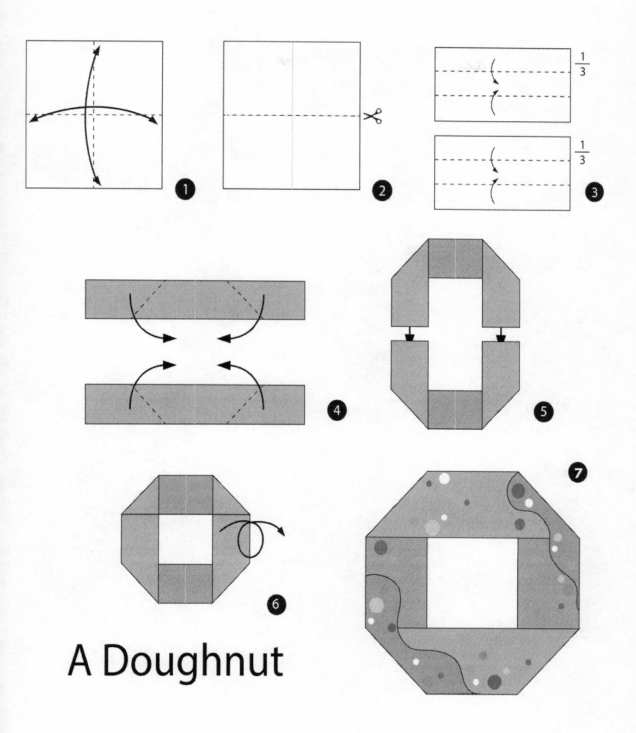

A Doughnut

LENGTH SAMURAI HAT

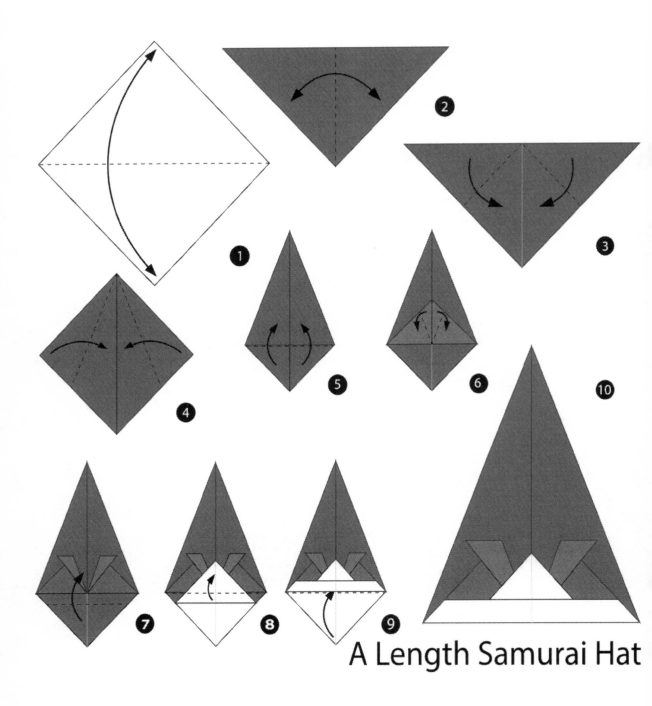

A Length Samurai Hat

LOLLYPOP

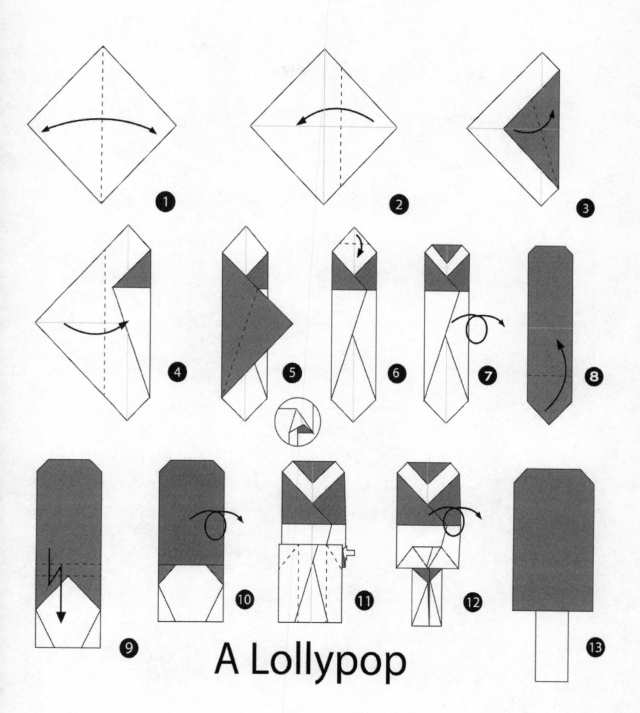

A Lollypop

DOG'S LETTER

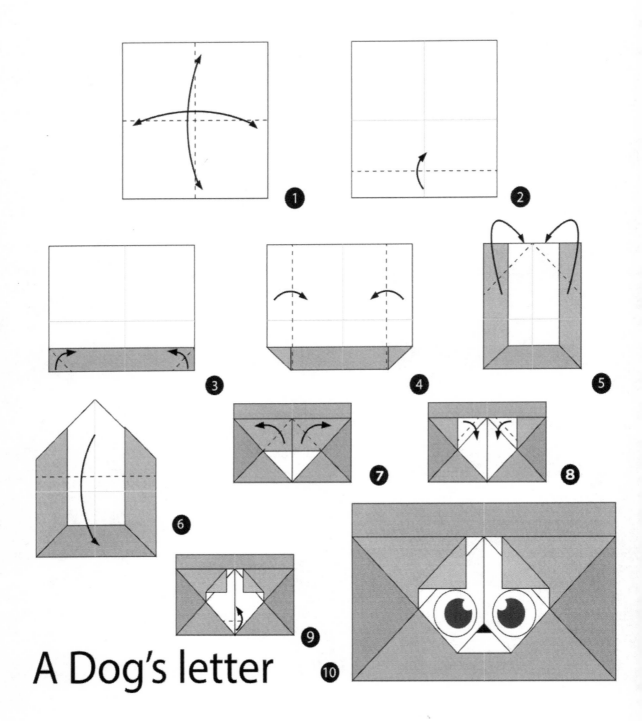

A Dog's letter

FAMILY HEART

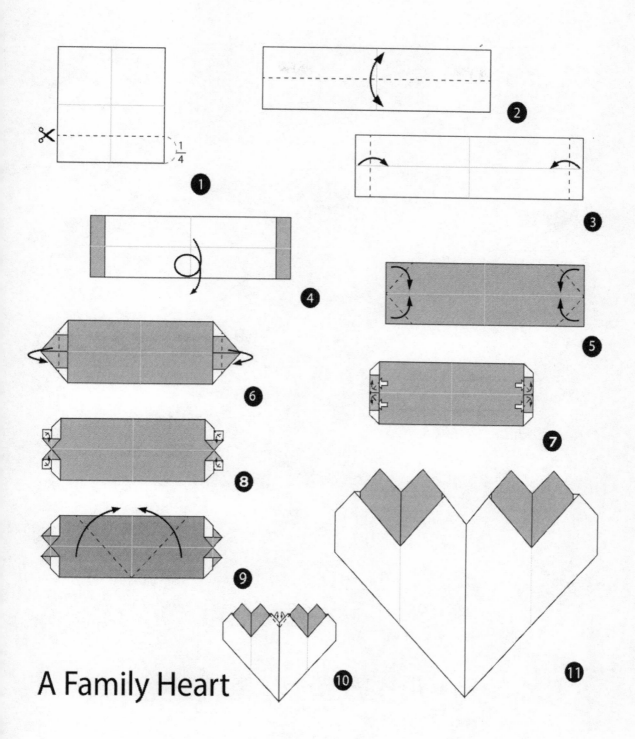

A Family Heart

BALLOON WITH WINGS

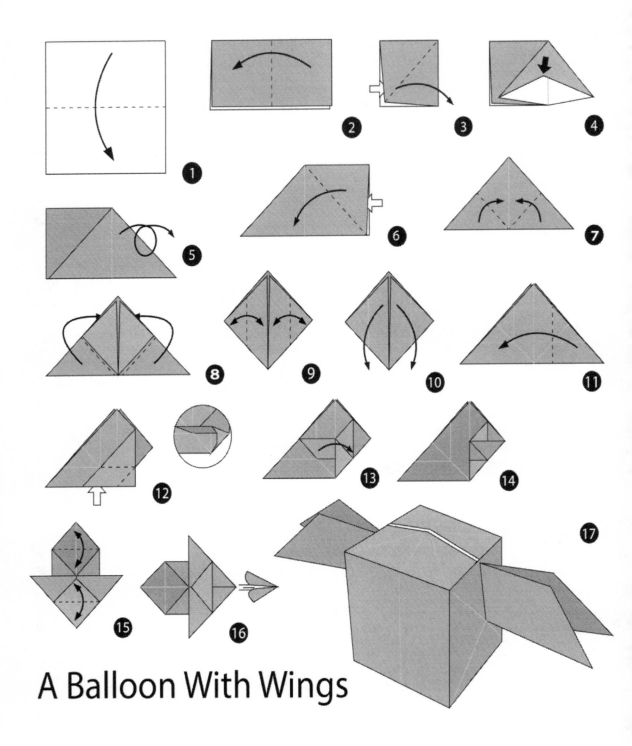

A Balloon With Wings

CAT

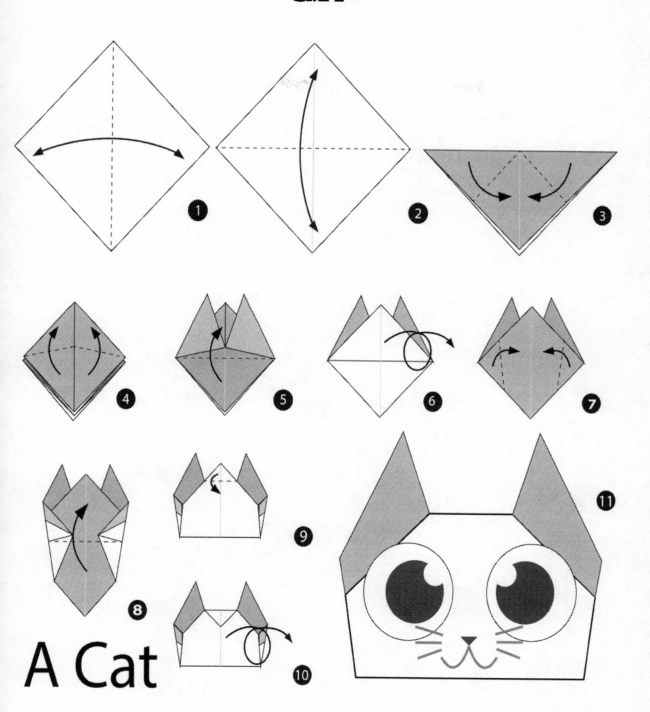

A Cat

GORILLA

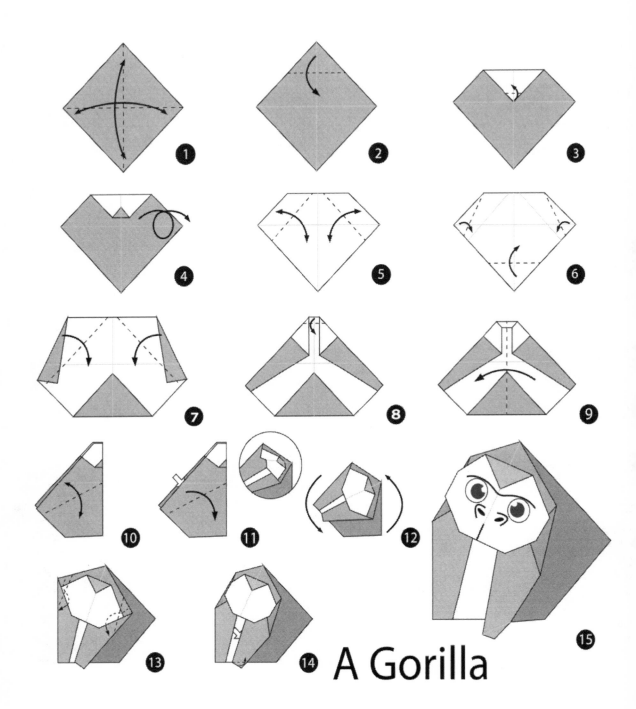

A Gorilla

GOLDFISH

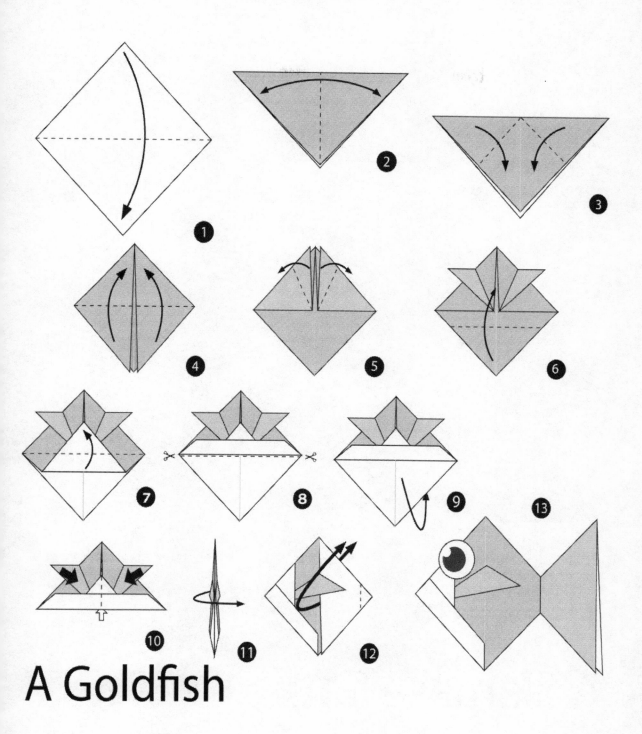

A Goldfish

SIAMESE CAT

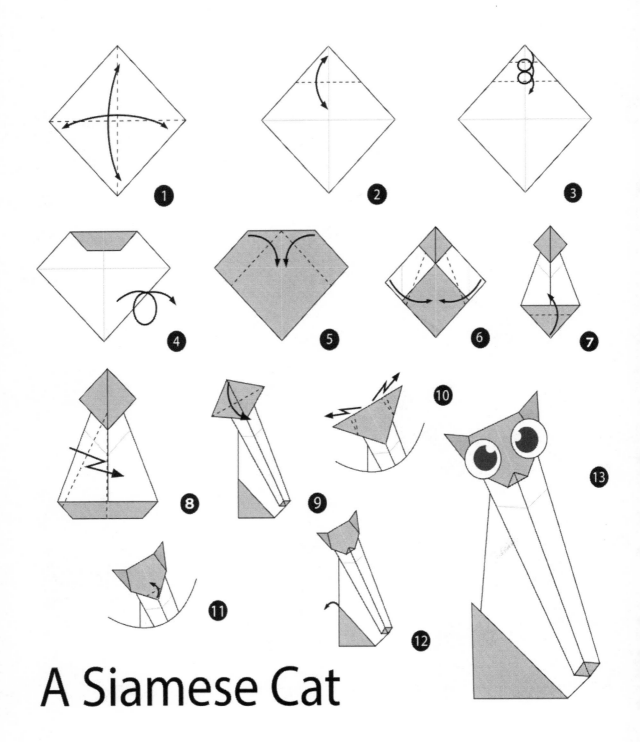

A Siamese Cat

PINEAPPLE

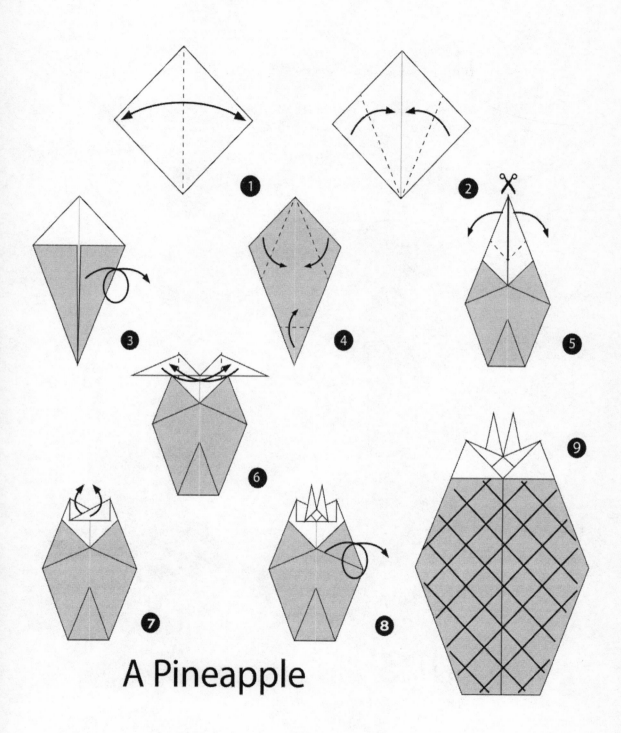

A Pineapple

PANSY

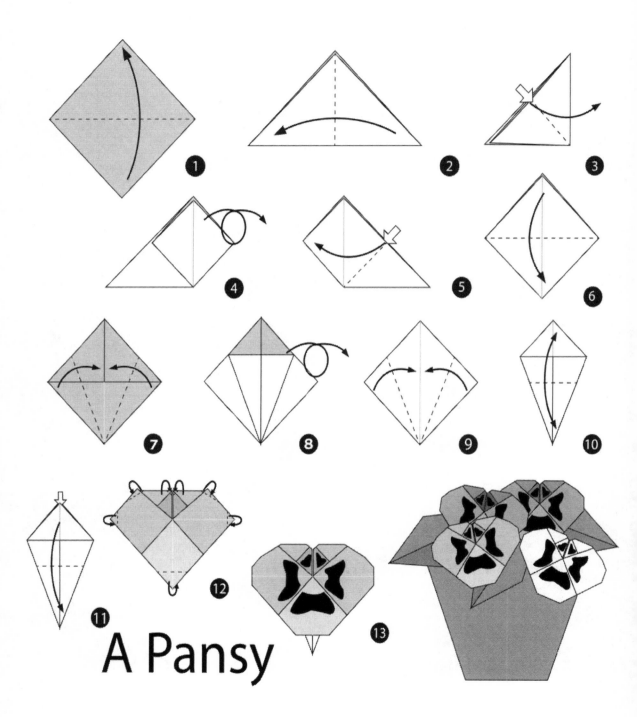

A Pansy

MUSHROOM

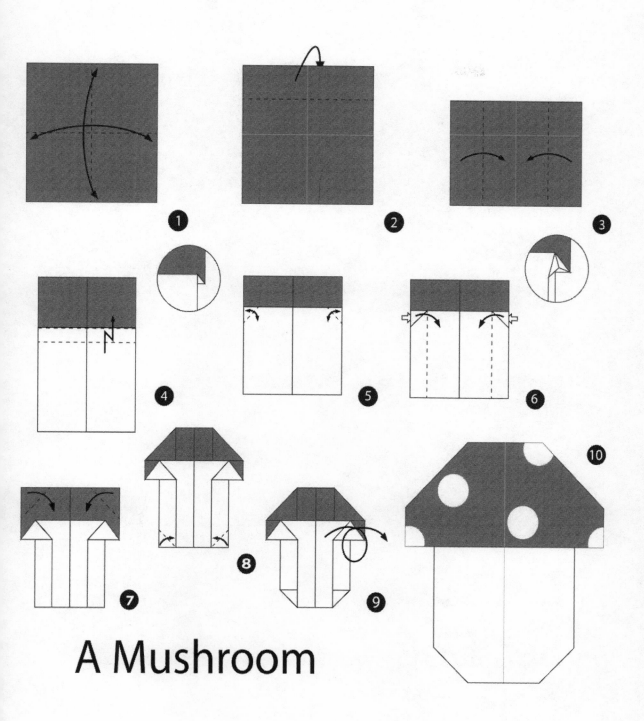

A Mushroom

SEA DOG

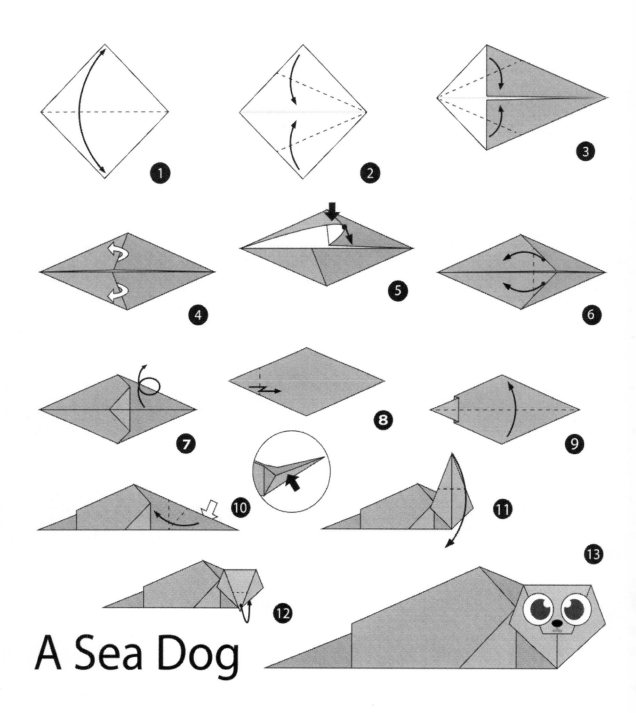

A Sea Dog

TWEETY BIRD

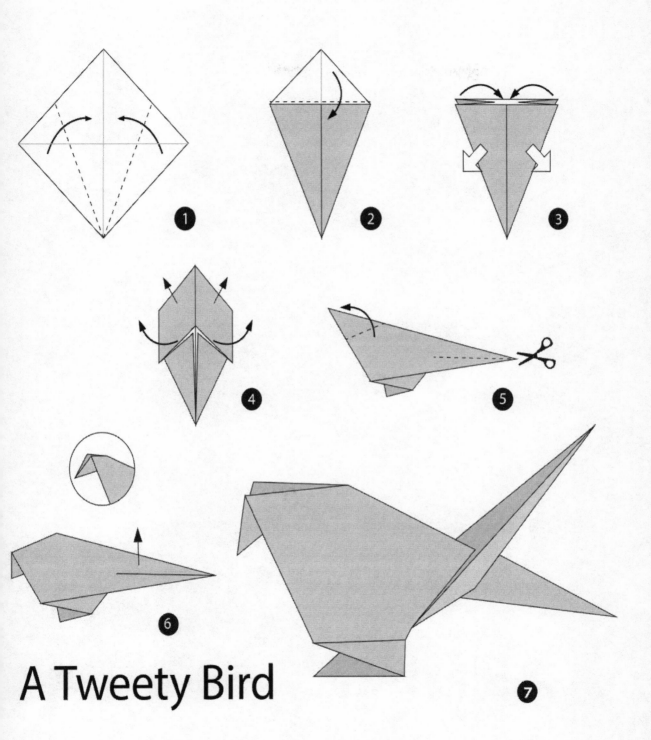

A Tweety Bird

BLACK CAT

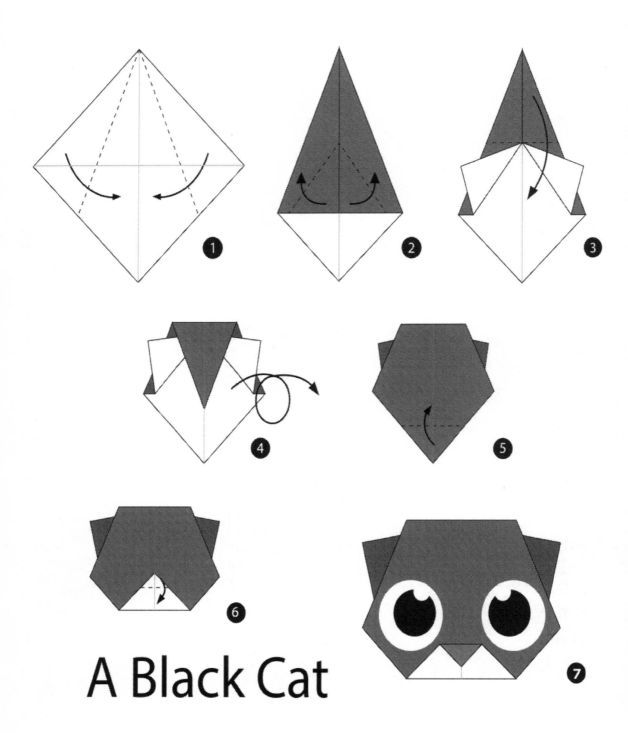

A Black Cat

SUNFLOWER

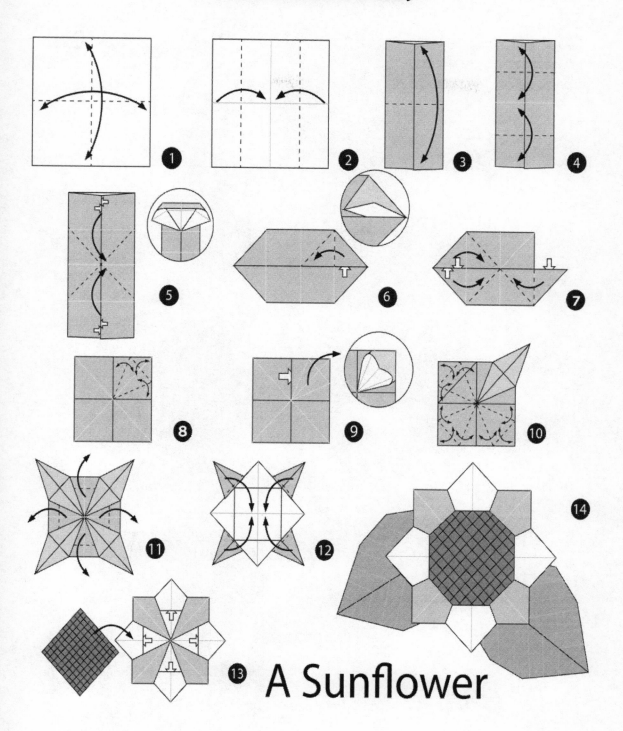

A Sunflower

COASTER

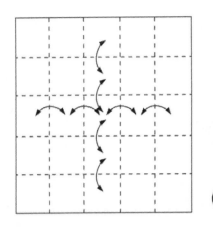

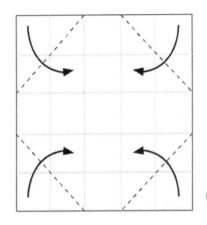

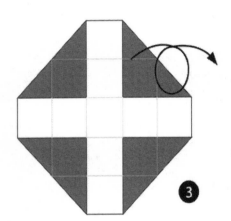

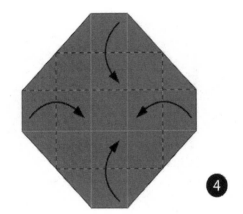

A Coaster

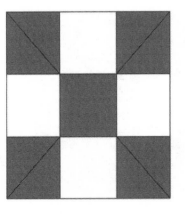

Made in the USA
San Bernardino, CA
08 May 2019